One Land, Many Cultures

Table of Contents

by Liz Ray

Getting Started

As Americans, we share the same homeland: the United States of America. We are all the same in many ways. But many of us have come from different backgrounds, or **cultures**. For example, immigrants who come here from other countries bring their special customs with them. And Native American groups have their own special **traditions**, too.

Over time, families pass their traditions on to their children and grandchildren. The traditions they share become part of their **heritage**.

Many people like sharing their traditions with others. We can all enjoy traditions from different cultures.

Art

Native Americans have produced art that many people enjoy. Art is more than just paintings and drawings. Art includes sculpture, weaving, pottery, and much more.

Navajo weavers make colorful rugs, blankets, and wall hangings. Their designs have been passed down for hundreds of years. Their weaving tradition is part of their heritage.

A sculptor, weaver, or potter
can make useful objects as well as
lovely works of art.

Many of the women who have
come from Laos pass on one of their
special traditions: how to embroider
clothing. They use colorful thread,
and they count stitches carefully.

Music

All over the world, people sing, chant, and make music. Immigrants and visitors bring their music to the United States. This new music now becomes part of the American culture.

Many familiar songs today began in other countries. One such song is "Yankee Doodle." British soldiers may have brought this song here from England in the 1700s.

Sometimes brand new music comes from old songs. For example, jazz came from early African-American music, such as work songs and other songs called *spirituals*.

Many jazz **musicians** and
singers still try to create new music.
The musicians make up music together
as they play their instruments.

Traditional music is often played at weddings and other celebrations. This is one way that people enjoy and pass on their musical heritage.

Dance

Along with music, dance is part of people's lives all over the world. Traditional dances are different from place to place. But most dances have something in common: the joy of movement!

In some dances, the movements are fast and lively. For example, a lively dance that came from Poland is called the *polka*. In other types of dances, the movements may be made slowly.

A dancer can be like an actor and use movement to tell a story. Dances can also help celebrate special times in people's lives.

The hula is an important dance in Hawaii. The dancers move to the music of traditional songs, or chants. Each movement has a special meaning. The hula helps Hawaiians feel proud of their heritage.

The lion dance is part of some Chinese celebrations in the United States and China. Dancers are inside the lion's head and body. They dance to drums and are often followed by crowds.

Literature

The best of the world's stories, poems, folktales, and other kinds of writing are all part of **literature**. Many of today's most popular stories began long ago. People would tell each other stories, and then the stories would be told over and over again to other people. Over time, writers would write down these stories.

Some stories may be similar in different countries. For example, the Cinderella story came from China. There are hundreds of retellings of this story all over the world.

People from many cultures have told stories about characters who play tricks. These stories are called *trickster tales*. Anansi the spider is a trickster in African stories. Coyote is a trickster in Native American tales.

One way we can enjoy each other's heritage is through literature. Now, think about your own heritage. What special traditions make you feel happy or proud? Which ones would you like to share with others?

Index